Lorraine

Legends
Stories and Cities of Lorraine

Order of Antrustions

Lorraine

Copyright © 2021 Order of Antrustions

All rights reserved.

ISBN: 9798551562665

Ancient and modern Lorraine Legends, Stories and Cities of Lorraine.

Lorraine

OBJECTIVES

To preserve the heritage of the Merovingian Bloodline and be a focal point of powerful ancient spiritual knowledge regarding the origin of Mankind on this planet, to collect this information from various sources and preserve this knowledge for future generations.

Publishing documents and ancient texts, organizing lectures in Stenay and organizing various excursions and travel arrangements to places of spiritual interest that are directly connected to the Merovingian Bloodline.

Lorraine

DEDICATION

Order of Antrustions

Vision

Order of Antrustion's vision is to re-establish our Western civilization based on Ancient Knowledge, Respect, Trust, Integrity, Service to Nature/Mankind and Acknowledgement of our Higher Connection/Origin.

Mission

To inform people of the Origin and True History of the Merovingian Bloodline, the Earth and the Spiritual Suppression that has been inflicted upon Mankind on this Planet to this day.

Real History

We gain tremendous power by understanding the truth about our history and the present. The truth does set us free from ignorance and suicidal acquiescence to present policies which are influential to the very fabric of our modern culture. If we examine what actually happened in the time called "the Dark Ages" we see a completely different picture than what history books want us to believe, that this era of retrogression was caused solely by "barbaric hordes."

The "Dark Ages" concept was largely brought on by corruption and the struggle for World Power by a New Religion.

Lorraine

PUBLICATIONS ORDER OF ANTRUSTIONS

Antrustions: The Bodyguards of Merovingian Kings.

Merovingian Notebook

Merovingian Crypte of Jouarre

Sigisbert III; Son of Dagobert I and Father of DagobertII

From Pharamond to Clovis

History of Dagobert II Son of Saint Sigisbert

Knight Templars, The Merovingian Connection

Sacred Merovingian Kings

Dagobert II: True origin of the House of Lorraine

Lorraine

CONTENTS

    Acknowledgments

1   The Legend of Lorraine

2   Arduinna

3   Stenay

4   Montmedy

5   Côte de Saint Germain/Jérusalem

6   Mont-Devant-Sassey

7   Lion-Devant-Dun

8   Juvigny-Sur-Loison

9   Saint Dagobert Fountain

10   Merovingian Facts

Lorraine

www.antrustions.com

The Founders of the Order of Antrustions all have in depth knowledge and interest in the Merovingian Bloodline. Knowledge that goes beyond the information that is available in general on the internet or other publications.

We sincerely hope you will enjoy our publications to expand your knowledge on this fascinating subject.

Lorraine

INTRODUCTION

The Early Middle Ages are commonly known as the 'Dark Ages', which portrays a time of decline, turmoil and darkness after the Romans left the Western European regions.

But in reality this was a prosperous time with many contacts/connections with other parts of the World. "We have to understand why there has been, till now, not much information available regarding this important period in our Western European History." This time was the decisive period in the establishment of the Holy Roman Catholic Church as the dominant Power in Europe for the next 1000 year.

The beginning of the Middle Ages, the Merovingian period, is mostly missing from the textbooks and it is thought that we know nothing about it. But a lot has been excavated in the Netherlands, Belgium and France regarding the times of the fifth to the seventh century. Spectacular gold treasures and rich grave fields full of personal luxury and status symbols such as jewelry, glassware and weapons show that this was a prosperous time.

Recent archaeological research of villages from the Early Middle Ages also yielded a lot of new information about how people lived, about housing construction, settlement patterns, early industry, rituals and identities.

Life in Merovingian Times appears to have been calmer and more prosperous than has always been thought, due to a favorable relationship between Land and People.

Lorraine

MEROVINGIAN STRUCTURE

Clovis (466-511 CE) was considered a King of the Salian Franks, but was also an official of the Romans. His conquest of other Kingdoms made him first of all a successful warlord. There was no governmental administration readily available to rule all these Kingdoms combined. The Merovingians acted pragmatically and took over much of the regional and locally existing systems of government after conquering these regions, to fit into a more global structure of government.

The change from pre-Merovingian government to Merovingian is perceptible in the capitularia, the legislation of the Kings. In the capitularia a distinction is made between more social strata of society than in the Lex Salica. The capitularia explicitly mention an elite which exercised a powerful influence and was treated differently then other people. These men will have come from the ancient Gallo-Roman senatorial families and the warlords that associated with Clovis and his sons in their conquest of Gaul. All held vast estates and possessed great wealth. From these families the King chose his officials, the bishops as a rule also came from these families. Added to the wealth of these families was thus political and religious power.

The Lex Salica indicates that Frankish society was originally governed by the meeting of important men of a region.

Government was small, because the productivity of farming seems to have been very low, not much above subsistence level. Therefore Kings, the Church and officials all had to deal with scarce resources for their sustenance. The labour force was limited in the sixth century because of the diminished population. And people had the possibility to move away when they felt oppressed by the government, as is mentioned in the Histories. For the elite, the possession of land was important for basic necessities such as food, accommodation and workers. But prosperity was

Lorraine

expressed more in the treasure that circulated among the elite by way of gifts or plunder, and less in the estates that were owned.

Because the Merovingian Kings did not pay most of their officials, only large landowners could afford to be officials. Most officials will have worked only part-time for the interests of the kingdoms, because they had to manage their own affairs too. Exceptions were officials who had no income of their own and who enjoyed the revenues of certain villages belonging to the royal treasury. Because they had their own means to organize, they got the assignment for public organization too. This system of government must have been decentralized to a large extent, with little rules.

Officials were appointed only for a period of time, from a pool of potential candidates. They had to have sufficient servants and warriors of their own to be able to exercise power. But when accepted as official by other magnates, an official could also call up other war bands and the militia of a civitas. Shifting coalitions could cause the withdrawal of this support and this would make another appointment necessary. An official was most of all a liaison in the region with the central authority. This cooperation could change to opposition when interests changed from those in the centre of power and only local support remained for the official. For the kings, the appointment of an official who was dependent on him was an attractive possibility to prevent such a situation. This was only possible when there was no agreement on a nomination for a position between the locals.

Officials did not receive regular payment for their work, but the position of an official had certain material advantages. Officials will have received gifts, as was an accepted custom, fines, rewards for arbitration, etc. In a society in which honour was an important asset, the higher social position of an official will have been important. Kings could make this even more distinctive by precious gifts, as symbols of power. Only the officials that were dependent on the king did receive an estate and other material support, to be able to occupy a position.

Lorraine

At the end of the sixth century, a growing coherence within the Kingdoms has resulted in a growing organization in taking care of the execution of several basic tasks, like taking care of war, taxes or gifts, arbitration, issuing of rules, international relations, registering property of land and estates, coinage, appointing officials, and confirming the election of bishops. In the capitularia there is a tendency towards rules for the public good, however theoretical these may have been because of a lack of means for execution of these rules.

The responsibilities of the government were small because there was a long tradition of self- government. Matters that are nowadays considered public affairs were dealt with privately, like the settlement of disputes by compensation or by feud, which were acceptable alternatives for arbitration by officials (Antrustions). It is also clear that many areas of care were outside the range where the government felt responsibility for. The poor, sick, widows and other vulnerable people, were not taken care of by the public administration. This was an assignment for the Church.

This all in all made the government very small.

Kings are certainly the most important persons in their Kingdom, central in the public administration, and all magnates tried to win their favour. But this perspective is an illusion created by Gregory because of his own interests and the interests of the Church. Gregory was in a position that depended largely on the support of a King. He needed a powerful King that could make his position as bishop stronger. But many of the actions of Kings, like Clovis using violence, betraying people, murdering, etc. were not very Christian, even though Gregory thought of Clovis as an ideal King. Many actions of Kings were in fact restricted by the power of coalitions of magnates or of collectives, like the army or the inhabitants of civitates.

Descent and reputation were the main ingredients for royal succession in Frankish society, as it will have been for the sons of magnates. According to the Lex Salica, all sons could inherit, but it was no rule to give all the heirs a share – let alone an equal share. A descent from Clovis was required when one wanted to become King. A Merovingian prince could be recognized as such by his father, other Merovingian Kings, sufficient magnates of a Kingdom, or the people. Gregory says that "irrespective of their mother's birth, all children born to a King count as that King's son". The implication of this is that, although the sons of a slave girl remained servile, when the father was a King the servility was ignored.

Preventing a man to become King could be achieved, apart from killing him; by calling this person a pretender, an illegitimate son, or by making a Prince incapable for the throne by shaving his head and making him a cleric.

A King could only rule with the help of a coalition of magnates. A weak King, for example, when he was a minor, could be ruled by a coalition of magnates, as was the case with King Childebert II and Chlothar II. Coalitions were loosely held together by the Merovingians Kings, who were in a way figureheads that could influence the course of a coalition only as leader of the largest war band, but were certainly not able to dictate its course.

A King was a symbol for unity of his Kingdom, but could be replaced if necessary by another Merovingian.

Lorraine

MÉROVÉE

Lorraine

ANTRUSTIONS

The "Trustis", warrior companionship, and the "Antrustion", voluntary companions of the Merovingian Kings of France, represented in Gaul a fundamental institution of the German conquerors and corresponded to one of the essential organs of the old Germanic society.

The Antrustions were held in the highest esteem and constituted the privy council, or general advisors to the King. Advocates were appointed from the ranks of the Antrustions by the King, to represent those people who were unable to represent themselves.

Lorraine

1

The Legend of Lorraine

The single rocks, the oddly formed stones, were objects of religious veneration during the period of the Gauls. They were seats of the ancient Gods, who received the devotion and homage from the faithful at these sites.

The stone of Milly, Menhir, near Dun-sur-Meuse, is one of the rare examples in Lorraine, a land which has been overrun too often by foreign invasions. If we are to believe the very ancient chroniclers, this stone, under the name of "Pierre Pertusa", (pierced stone), was formerly used as the frontier marker between the Merovingian Kingdoms of Austrasie and Neustria.

It is also known under the name of "Hotte du Diable" (the Devils Sack), because in the imagination of the primitive Christians, when substituting the gods of paganism with Satan, and confusing them with the same disapproval. They considered that this stone was undoubtedly a place of pagan worship and of diabolical origin.

Lorraine

All this happened a very long time ago when the gods of the Gallo-Roman pantheon had been usurped in favor of the single God of the Christians.

Saint Saintin had evangelised Verdun and with great difficulty Saint Remacle, the apostle of the Ardennes, had chased from the Forest of the Woevre all the Satyrs, Priapi and Valkyries that had chosen to make their homes there since time immemorial. So Satan, powerless, saw his fortresses fall, one after the other. He no longer knew where to take refuge. He did not dare approach the places sanctified by the new Faith. But he was tenacious and would not admit defeat.

Lorraine

So he resolved to make one last supreme effort to take back his old Kingdom and his power.

Above all, he wanted to find the place where the monks of Saint Remacle had establish themselves at Stavelot in Walloon country. He blamed them for all his misfortune and decided to annihilate them. He uprooted a mountain of granite, fixed a large brass ring around it and loaded it onto his shoulders in a sack. He went down into the valley of the Meuse, avoiding Verdun, access to which had been forbidden to him since the arrival of Saint Saintin. His intention was to crush the monastery under an enormous mass of rock.

The "Smoking King" went alone slowly, bent under his burden, which squashed his shoulders. But anger and the certainty of delivering a decisive blow to his enemies increased his strength tenfold.

Meanwhile, his passage spread flames and sulphur everywhere. So he cleared the places that he crossed by fire, scorching the marshy grasslands, burning the impenetrable forests. So he implemented the "slash and burn", rendering valuable services to the future inhabitants of these lands without being aware of it. But Saint Remacle was warned of the danger which threatened the monastery and without hesitation was determined to oppose the Devil's disastrous design.

Clothed in a cowl, armed with his pilgrim's staff, he went out to meet him. On his back he carried a sack, into which he had all the old sandals of his monks. He soon joined up with the devil in the region of Stenay. Exhausted by his long walk and by the weight of his charge, the demon had thrown the rock onto the ground and was sitting on top of it. His brown skin ran with phosphorescent sweat and his breath smelled of burning sulphur. He peered closely at the horizon, looking to see where he should go.

Soon he saw an old man with a scrawny look, who was drinking and he too was carrying a sack, the weight of which appeared to crush him. It was Saint Remacle, but Satan didn't recognize him.

When he was within hearing distance Satan got up and went towards him; greetings old stranger.

Without getting up, Saint Remacle returned his greetings.

Lorraine

-*"Where are you going like that then"*, asked the Devil, who wanted to engage him in a conversation to find out the exact place where the stronghold of his enemy could be found.

-*"To Rome"*, replied Saint Remacle.

-*"That's a very long way away, indeed"*, replied Satan.

-*"And you, where are you going, you seem to be worn out"*, continued the Saint.

-*"I'm going to Stavelot, but tell me old man, is it still far to go"?*

-*"My poor friend, it is far away, very far away still. I know because I come from there"*.

-*"Anyway, look at my sack. I have used all these sandals since I left that town"*.

-*"What"? Said the Devil, seeing the impressive number of sandals that were crammed into the sack.*

-*"So it is still so far away"?*

-*"Alas, yes"*, replied Saint Remacle.

With these words the Devil realized that he would never get to the Monastery with his load. A terrible anger took hold of him and in his rage he seized the rock, pulled the ring from it and threw the enormous mass into the air. The stone made a great arc in the sky as far as the horizon and it fell to earth a long way from there, in the middle of the plain of Dun-Sur-Meuse.

That's how it earned its name!

Lorraine

2

Arduinna

In early Merovingian religion, Arduinna was the goddess of Lakes, Rivers and Springs, also of Fruit and Vegetables.

She was often called the Lady of the Lake.

Arduinna was already worshipped by the Sicambrians, precursors of the Franks who would later become the Merovingians. The Sicambrians were also called the people of the bear, because of their worship of the bear goddess. The Ardennes was the sacred forest of the goddess Arduinna, who is equated with Diana. The Ardennes were named after her.

She was a goddess of the forest and of the hunt. She rode through the woods on her horse, accompanied by her retinue, which included dogs. She was also depicted riding a male pig. The pig was of great importance in Celtic religion.

Devena is sometimes believed to be traced back to Diana, but is probably an older form of the same goddess who was the basis for the Roman Diana. She also corresponds to virgin Greek hunting goddesses such as Artemis and her alter egos. The Slavic forms of her name can be associated with the word "virgin"; the meaning of Arduinna is also explained as "Most High.

The bear is an ancient symbol, originating in Greek Arcadia. It was in the coat of arms of the Royal House of Arcadia.

In 585, St. Wolfroy preached to the local population of Villers-devant-Orval in the Ardennes to persuade them to abandon the worship of Diana. On the hill near Margut, there was, according to Gregory of Tours, a large stone statue of Diana where people would come for worship. Worshippers would also sing chants in Diana's honour as they drank and feasted.

Lorraine

3

Cities and Places of Lorraine

Stenay

Situated to the North-West of the Forest of Woevre, on the right bank of the Meuse, in the middle of a catchment area fed by the waters of this river and the Canal l'Est, this town was always an important strategic site. The entrance point from the North-East to France.

This place which was already known about in Celtic times and was an oppidum in Roman times was desirable because of its important location on the Meuse, at the entrance to the Forest of Woevre. Thierry, son of Clovis, who became King of Austrasie, was struck by the position of Stenay, and had a palace built there. The village of Stenay became the *Villa Regia* (the Royal Town) and the County town. Thierry, his son, and his grandson were buried in the Castle Chapel. In his time Dagobert II lived here.

In the 10th Century, Stenay belonged to the House of Ardennes. It then became in the possession of the Duke of Bouillon. On leaving for the crusade, Godefroy de Bouillon sold the town (the only place not part of the sale, which he kept was the site where the Merovingian King Dagobert II was buried) together with the Château that he had built. In 1077 it went to the Bishop of Verdun, who gave it to the Count of Luxembourg in 1110. The Count sold Stenay to Renaud, Count of Bar and until 1641 it remained almost continuously in the possession of the House of Bar, then of Lorraine.

From 1609 to 1611, new fortifications were built and it became an important strategic place again. In 1646 Louis XIV gave the property to the Prince de Conde. As the Prince had gone over to the Spanish side, the King gave orders for it to be besieged. Faubert undertook this in 1654 in the presence of the King himself. The siege lasted for 56 days. Eventually in 1659, by the Treaty of the Pyrenees, the King gave Stenay to Faubert. The city ramparts were dismantled in 1689. His descendants enjoyed their patronage until the French Revolution.

In 1790 it was the County town of a district consisting of 75 town councils. The city withstood the Austrian siege in 1792 and was occupied by the Germans during the whole of the first Great War (1914-1918). The Crown Prince Wilhelm had his headquarters in Stenay.

After his assassination in 679, the body of King Dagobert II was buried in the basilica of Saint Rémi of Stenay. The Royal tomb was rediscovered in 872 and the Church fathers listed his devout monarch among the number of Saints and Martyrs of the faith.

Spurred on by the Carolingian King, Charles the Bald, a new Church was built on the site of the old Basilica of Saint Rémy, as well as a monastery at Juvigny-sur-Loison. These two buildings were placed under the patronage of Saint Dagobert.

In the 17th Century it was decided to rebuild the Citadel in Stenay on a new foundation and the ancient Church of Saint Dagobert was ruthlessly subjected to successive re-development imposed by the military architects. The access route to the Citadel passes through the Church grounds, the walls of which were buried. The Church was mentioned again at the beginning of the 20th Century, but it completely disappeared after the First Great War of 1914-1918.

In 1965, during works undertaken on his property, Monsieur Laplante, the architect at Stenay, discovered ancient walls, which led him to believe that this was the gateway of the Church of Saint Dagobert.

Lorraine

In 1972, a group of Stenay citizens known as the "Group" for the research and improvements of historic documents, led by Monsieur Renault, Professor at the Stenay Lycée, embarked on the updating of the gateway. The showpiece is the sculpted tympanum probably representing Saint Dagobert seated in majesty, flanked by two people on their knees. The gateway was dismantled systematically into separate pieces and stored in the Church of Sacré-Cœur.

Lorraine is not well-endowed with historical monumental art. From the Roman period we know only of four tympani: Laitre-sous-Amance, the Lion gateway at Verdun, Pompierre and Vomecourt-sur-Madon.

The transition from the Roman to the Gothic dates the gateways of *Notre Dame de Nancy*, (in the Lorraine Museum of History), *Saint Eucaire Liverdun* (around 1200), *Lemencourtt* (beginning of the 13th Century) and *Gorze*.

Gateway of Dagobert

The Saint Dagobert remembrance room in Stenay attracts visitors from all over the world. They are interested in the history of the Merovingian Dynasty, and Stenay (Especially the history of Dagobert II).

Lorraine

Throughout history, and especially in the last Century we have seen many publications regarding this period in time, but it was the publication of "LA RACE FABULEUSE" in 1973 by Gerard de Sede which developed a renewed interest for the Merovingian history, in particularly that of King Dagobert II.

These publications have dealt mostly with thé mysteries of Rennes-le-Château in the South of France at the end of the 19th Century, revolving around the descendants of King Dagobert II. This little village was the stronghold of Sigisbert IV, the son of King Dagobert II.

You can find pictures and a short video of the remembrance room in Stenay, the gateway and the replica of the Mysterious Stone on our Antrustions website and YouTube channel.

The Mysterious Stone

We believe that the mysterious stone could be explained as a Christian *gesture,* at a time when there were not many Christians in Stenay. It should be remembered that all the sculpted stones found in Stenay were discovered in the foundations of the Basilica of Saint Rémi. This was the building which existed on this site prior to the Church of Saint Dagobert, which replaced it in the 9th Century.

These stones, which were re-used in the foundation, were funeral stèles. The one we are talking off is a particular type. The late Mr. M. Plantard studied this stèle while working on the history of Stenay. He thought that the letters engraved on the left, and the chevron marked on the right of these letters were a "key" allowing Initiates to refer to the famous "Sator Square ".

To illustrate; this famous stone has been reproduced, as you can see on our YouTube channel. Some letters have been deliberately emphasized. These letters "SRNPR" in their proper places in the square, trace exactly the line of the chevron engraved on the replica.

The Sator Square contains 5 words, which can be read in all ways: SATOR, AREPO, TENET, OPERA, ROTAS. The pagans, who used the stone before the Christians, placed the word: ROTAS at the top, instead of the word SATOR (as in Pompeii).

This inversion of the two words does not change the meaning:

Lorraine

The Creator: (SATOR), we will pass on AREPO, which only has a meaning when said in reverse, holds (TENET) the wheels, (ROTAS) with care. In other words: he who has made, who has "sown" (life, mankind, the world), oversees and directs his course carefully. And for the Christians: The creator of mankind is also "Providence".

Significance of the Stone of Stenay

The occult nature of this stele suggests that it was engraved at a time when Christians could not show themselves openly. It is dated at approximately the 5th Century or the beginning of the 6th Century, when there was an upsurge of pagan zeal after the "conversion" of Clovis in 496.

Unfortunately the original sand stone of Stenay is no longer at Stenay. Around 1910 Mr. Rivart deposited the stone with Mgr. Mangin, who died in 1914 and did not witness the removal of the stone by the unduly famous German Crown Prince Wilhelm, son of Kaiser Wilhelm II, who had its headquarters in Stenay, who smashed it, and then declared; I am the Master of the Cross!

Once again, a monument of great historical value disappeared.

The reconstruction of the "Stone of Stenay" is on display in the crypte of Dagobert.

```
SÀTOR
AREPO
TENET
OPERA
ROTAS
```

This stone, discovered at Stenay and bearing the four engraved letters and the chevron, can be identified by comparing it with the tile of

Lorraine

Acquineuem in Budapest, which was discovered in 1935, and to other "squares" found in Pompeii and at several other European sites.

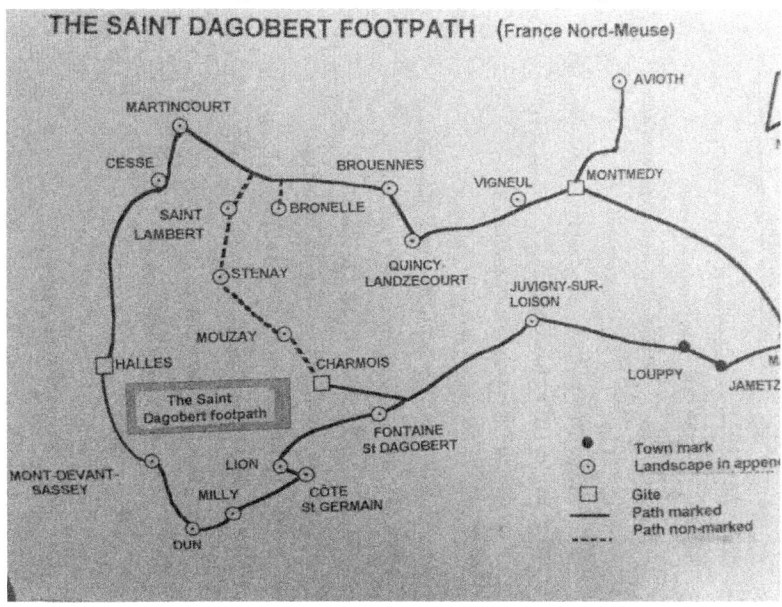

Lorraine

4

Montmedy

Located on the Chiers, where the roads to Vouziers-Longuyon and Sedan-Metz meet, you will find the town Montmedy, the former Capital of the Counts of Chiny.

Dom Calmet, in his *Notice on Lorraine,* wrote: "It seems that Montmedy has taken its name from it being located between the Château of Jametz and La Frette, as to its surrounding walls, it resembles an unequal triangle, with a blunted point. It's base faces East, the shortest side faces South and the longest side faces North. Instead of ending in a point, it's Westward extremity consists of two neighboring bastions. One is called the bastion des Connils and is near the Château, the other is the bastion de Saint Andre. The town of Montmedy is situated between these mountains."

Lorraine

Montmedy is divided between the high town and the low town. The high town has a square with a Church, a town hall, the former sub-prefecture and several houses. It is surrounded by walls built in the 17th Century by the Chevalier de Ville et Vauban and dominates the Valleys of the Chiers, the Thonne and the Othain. The river Chiers flows through the low town, which is from a more recent date.

In the middle of the 6th Century, there was a temple dedicated to Mercury on the heights of Montmedy. Several centuries later the Counts of Chiny established a hunting lodge there and in 1239 Arnould de Chiny laid the foundations of the town, which became the capital of the County of Chiny.

Montmedy then later passed into the houses of Burgundy in 1444, Austria in 1477 and Spain in 1555.

Montmedy withstood a memorable siege in 1657. During the 2 months long siege, Louis XIV personally tried to reduce the city. Montmedy was defended by the commander Jean d'Alamont de Malandry and 736 men, after he was mortally wounded, the garrison capitulated. The King lost 5800 men during the siege. Montmedy was ceded to France in 1659 by the treaty of the Pyrenees on November 9th.

Between 1790 and 1870, Montmedy was an important strategic site. It withstood two other memorable sieges in 1815 and 1870. During the Great War, it was taken on 29th August 1914 and liberated on September 19th 1918.

There are four churches to see in Malmedy:

Notre-Dame d'Ire-les-Pres
Saint-Martin de Fresnois
St-Bernard de la Ville Basse
St-Martin de la Ville Haute

Lorraine

Entrance to Montmedy.

Avioth

Avioth is a village of 152 inhabitants situated 7 km from Montmedy in the valley of the river Thonne. After the 12th Century a sanctuary was built to house a statue of the Virgin that was famous for its miracles. Tradition has it that Saint Bernard came there on a pilgrimage in 1131. The actual building is dated to the first part of the 14th Century (Champenois Gothic), but the works were carried out over a Century and by the time the building was finished it was the year 1420. At the beginning of the 15th century the famous was built at the entrance to the cemetery in 1539 a Chappell in flamboyant style watch added to the south transept from 1560 the church was used as a refuge by the inhabitants fleeing from the army rebel it was also pillaged several times until the treaty of the Pyrenees on 1659 which brought calm into the region. The church which was restored in the 19th century consists of a nave with three spans of unequal dimension, flanked with simple aisles. There is a choir down one

Lorraine

aisle and at the end, a pentagonal apse around which there is an ambulatory containing three chapels, lodged against the flying buttresses.

On the outside, the South face has been modified by the construction of the chapel of Saint John the Baptist. In this part there is a very fine gateway topped by a gable. The buttresses were formerly crowned with pinnacles up as far as the flamboyant sculptures. Unfortunately, the central gateway, which is decorated with a rose, and is still very beautiful, was damaged during the French Revolution. The statues of Saints and Characters from the Bible, which adorned it, were destroyed or decapitated. The two short towers, supported by the flying buttresses, have windows on two floors.

There is some very interesting furniture in the Church. In the choir, enclosed by an elegant 15th Century stone railing, the main altar is worth looking at, as are the seat of the celebrant, a 12th Century statue of the Virgin and Child, the 15th Century tomb of Catherine de Breux, Lady of Avioth, several funerary monuments in the ambulatory, some 14th p, 18th Century statues, e renaissance pulpit of 1538, the organ case of 1715 and the stalls of the sculptor Bandeville de Stenay, dating from 1784.

The "Recevresse" in front of the cemetery was financed by the Rodemack family. It is a cage 14 metres high, set on round columns and covered by a vault of pointed arches divided I to 6 compartments. The buttresses topped by pinnacles are connected by a high balustrade, all in the purest flamboyant style. It is thought that this unique building was used to collect donations in coin and in kind from the pilgrims. The main pilgrimage is held every year on the 16th July.

Legend has it that some shepherds discovered a wooden statue, representing the Virgin Mary in a bush of the horns. They took it to a neighboring Church. The following day the statue had gone back to its thorn bush. The mother of god obviously wanted to have a sanctuary build on this spot.

Lorraine
_____

Lorraine

5

Côte de Saint-Germain/Jérusalem

At an altitude of 352 metres, the Côte de Saint-Germain is the highest point in the County, one part of the hill is known as the Côte de Saint-Germain, named after the famous Mystic, the other part is known as Jerusalem, it most probably got this name in ancient times, around the times of Godfried de Bouillon. It is part of the Eastern chain of hills that border the Meuse for the length of the department. It's peak is quite isolated.

At the top of this mount an oppidum called Hadrians camp is to be found, this was the name of the 2th Century Roman emperor, who reigned in the middle of the 2th Century AD, about 500 years before Dagobert II. A few Centuries earlier, the Celtic Gauls had surrounded this peak with a fortification.

It has the form of a semicircle, rising like an amphitheatre: vines used to cover its flanks for two third of its height. In 1860 phylloxera destroyed the whole of this vineyard.

A road rises along the side of the Cote de Saint-Germain, leading to its summit, which forms a plateau of 20 hectares. It was formerly deciduous woodlands on its South-West flanks. These are now forested with pines.

There was said to have been a chapel at the North-Eastern extremity, a primitive Church, which then became a hermitage and later on, a cemetery. This is indicated in documents in the State archives of 1698. The priest' responsibility for the office continued until 1792. The cemetery existed until 1700, when bits of bones, medals and ancient coins were found at a shallow depth, almost at the surface. A cross indicates the spot today, as well as a hedge, which surrounds it.

Lorraine

Midways, almost opposite the site of the hermitage, 200 metres to the West, a cavi, or a small cellar, built of stone, can be found. At the bottom of this cavi, the water from the sloping side flows into an extensive stonelined excavation of about 10 cubic metres in volume, forming an artificial spring. This cavi and spring are the remains of the hermitage of Saint-Germain.

This cavi was a work of ingenuity carried out by our ancestors, who were devoted to the hermitage. It still exists and is worth our respect as well being kept in repair. It is also worth visiting as much for its historic interest as it is for being a tourist attraction. The hermit came there to fetch his water, the access path to the hermitage can still be seen.

The church of Lion possesses an overhang coming from the hermitage of Saint-Germaine, listed by the "Fine arts" department. It was found in the forges of Orval and is very ancient.

Close to the hermitage, to the West, is a small mound or tumulus called"Multi". There is a historical tradition that following a battle, the Romans buried their dead with the arms in a tomb there. Remains of arms, medals, bones and buildings have been found in this location.
The last occupant of the hermitage of Saint-Germain was called: Brother Raulin. He died at the forge in Stenay on 17th November 1777.

From this vantage point the panoramic view of the landscape is quite breathtaking.

Lorraine

Sion-Vaudemont

Sion-Vaudemont known in French as the colline inspiree, was first a Centre of Celtic worship for over 2000 years before he Roman period and then during the Merovingian period, this horseshoe-shaped Hill continued to be a Centre of worship for thousands of years, even today pilgrimage continues to come to the Church of Notre-Dame-de-Sion (attributed to Mary-Magdalene)

Grant

Grant, this small village situated in Southern Lorraine sits above the once healing sanctuarium of the Celtic God Grannus. During the Merovingian times this town was known as Gallum, it also houses Roman built aqueducts, basilica and an Amphi-Theater which could hold 20.000 people.

There is a magnificent and well preserved mosaic pavement, dating from the first century.

Lorraine

Lorraine

Dun-Sur-Meuse

Dominating the valley of the Meuse, Dun is an oppidum which was converted to a stronghold around 1053 by Godefroy IV, Count of Verdun. It became the headquarters of the barony, then of the county and finally of the military police. The Church is the only building that remains of the high town, which was destroyed during the 1914-1918 war. The Château had already been dismantled in 1642 by order of Louis XIII. Only Dun-bas (Lower Dun) remains. The Church, dedicated to Notre-Dame, was built around 1350, thanks to the generosity of Geoffroy d'Apremont, Lord of Dun and his wife, Marguerite de Sully.

The five-span nave, with aisles on either side, is followed by a transept, a choir, a span and a five-sided apse. The gateway opens onto a porch surrounded by two chapels. The bell tower was reconstructed in the 16th Century. The furnishings are interesting. Among them are some funerary epitaph fragments of a 15th Century stone altarpiece; a pulpit to preach from and the main altar is from the 18th Century.

Lorraine

6

Mont-Devant-Sassey

This was a continuation of the chapter of the nobleladies of Andenne in Belgium, from a very ancient time, the 7th Century at least. The Church is one of the finest in the Verdun region, and was built at the end of the 12th Century. The apse, the very wide choir, the transept and some walls of the nave date from our period. The nave itself has four spans and the aisles were finished in the 13th Century. The gateway on the south aisle and the two towers of the chevet were added then. The bell tower porch dates from the 14th Century.

In the 17th Century the Church was put on a defensive footing and withstood a siege from which it emerged in a very damaged stage. It was necessary to reconstruct the vaults of the nave first, and then, in 1754, the porch. Restored in 1869, it was repaired again in 1928. Under the choir and the apse there is a Crypt worthy of note with three naves, the Roman columns of which are decorated with wide-open capitals, which are reminiscent of those of the Verdun Cathedral.

The gateway has kept its statuary, although unfortunately they are very damaged. The Virgin to hom the Church was dedicated has disappeared, but figures from the Old and New testament still exist. The nativity occupies the lintel. On the tympanum can be seen the scenes recounting the childhood of Christ, the Apostles etc.

Lorraine

Halles-Sous-les-Côtes

Situated on the bank's of the Meuse, it is a village that is one of the most typical and best preserved of the region of Stenay. It flourished until the 19th Century and traces of its prosperity remain. It's Church, it's l'avoir/drinking trough and the houses of its wine-growers and peddlers remain as witnesses to a period unfortunately long gone.

It was the iron mine of Halle, which provided the iron ore for the foundries of Stenay. They were closed in 1847.

Halle-Sous-Les- Côtes is the original departure point of the traditional pilgrimage of Notre Dame de Montserrat, which takes place every year at the beginning of September. A statue of this Catalan Virgin is situated in a grotto by the side of a miraculous spring. Numerous walks are possible among the gardens and the nearby spring.

Lorraine

Thionville

City of passage, Thionville is also a very coveted border city. Situated on a linguistic and therefore cultural boundary between Roman and Francique languages, it is also a political boundary that is constantly being questioned.
The first permanent human settlement of farmers was not before the 5th millennium. Although the city has very few traces of the Gallo-Roman period, the Moselle valley played a major role due to the presence of numerous Roman legions along the Rhine and the establishment of Trier as an imperial residence.

The first mention of the city under the name of Theodonis Villa, a form from which derives both Thionville and its Germanic form Diedenhofen, dates back to 753. Around 770, the presence of a palatium publicum was reported, which seems to have been appreciated by the Carolingian rulers (Charlemagne, Louis the Pious, Lothaire 1st, Louis the Germanic).

Lorraine

Cesse

The village of Cesse had been part of the Departmentof the Ardennes until 1821. The Church, is of recent construction (1893), possesses an ancient piece of furniture. The village was badly damaged by the battles of the Great War (1914-1918) but has been able to preserve its former settlement (farms, mill, school). The mill is at the centre of the village. It is a fine building we're the stream is bringing the water to it, and the little dam makes this place a magnificent spot.

Lorraine

Martincourt-Sur-Meuse

A parish formerly attached to Stenay, the little village of Martincourt was completely destroyed in 1940, as was its neighbor, Inor. The little chapel only dates from 1953-1956.

Water flows from a great many springs in hillsides, which dominate the village and the Valley of the Meuse.

There are walks on the plateau, which has several viewing points, and in the Valley, along the Meuse and the canal de l'est.

Lorraine

7

Lion-Devant-Dun

In 1706 the Church of Lion-Devant-Dun consisted of the nave and the choir. The Church is very spacious and a fine building, bearing in mind the size of the former population of the parish.

At the head of the magnificent entrance door to the sanctuary is the inscription "DOMUS DEI", the House of God. The choir has a wealth of costly listed statues and it's ceiling is decorated with paintings depicting heaven, purgatory and hell. In the transept under the vault, the beam of glory is decorated with ancient statues of Mary Magdalene on the right, Saint Anne on the left and Christ in grande style, in the centre, fastened onto a huge cross, everything in keeping with the beam of glory. Other listed items include a statue of Saint. Maur, a sculpted pulpit and fountain, which is a relic from the hermitage of Saint-Germain. The Church is Roman in style and supported by buttresses. After it was built, the village dipped into its resources and sixty years later, in 1756, the Church tower was added by the Medar brothers, who were builders in Lion. The stone, which is very hard, came from the quarries of Saint-Germain, extracted by MM. Hazard, quarry owner in Lion.

Above the tower entrance door, in a medallion, surrounded by angels, engraved on the stone, is the inscription:

"ANNO DOMINI MDCCLXXVI"

From 1700 to 1854 there was a cemetery next to the Church, which was known as the Saint Maur cemetery. In 1854, after the cholera epidemic, a new cemetery was created about 250 metres from the Church and was named after the first person to be buried in it; the Saint-Claude cemetery. The entrance gate was made by Monsieur Petitpas, a wrought iron

Lorraine

craftsman from Lion. At its head the inscription: "Porta Vitae" (Gate of Life). It is adorned by two walnut trees, one on the right and one on the left, both planted in 1859.

In 1892, the local council planted lime trees around the former cemetery of Saint Maur out of respect for this sacred place and for the 2,274 ancestors buried there. The original Church dates from the 6th Century and was dedicated to Saint Martin, the country's mother Church. Saint Wandrille probably gave it to the monks of Montfaucon who changed its name to Saint Germain, their patron Saint.
A pilgrimage in honour of the Saint was soon established on the hill-top. The Church was then entrusted to a hermit until the révolution came.

The Church has a beautiful window with a scene of Dagobert II.

———————————————————————

Lorraine

Mouzay

The Church of Mouzay is especially interesting for the quality and diversity of its stainless glass windows. They are not old, dating from the beginning of the 20th Century. The window representing Dagobert II is of special interest, it marks his entrance to the forest, the scene of his assasination.

Each year the pilgrims of Saint Dagobert assemble in the Church of Mouzay, where a ceremony is held. After the ceremony they then leave the Church on foot along the forest footpaths for the fountain of Saint Dagobert. A stop is organised at the Château of Haut Charmois.

Lorraine

8

Juvigny-Sur-Loison

The village of Juvigny gets its name from an ancient agricultural estate of the Roman-Gallo period. The foundation of the Abbey in 872 relates to the discovery of the tomb of Saint Dagobert II in the Church of Saint Rémy in Stenay. The Church of Saint Dagobert, which replaced it, as well as the monastery of Juvigny, founded by Charles the Bald and Queen Richilde.

The religious community received the relics of Saint Dagobert and placed them with those of Saint Benedict and his sister, Saint Scholastica, , which they already possessed.

The history of these relics has been closely linked to that of the village of Juvigny and it's monastery from its foundation. They have been through all the wars and invasions, which his little village of Lorraine has known.

In fact, the relics of Saint Scholastica are still kept in the village Church and have always been an object of pilgrimage. The Abbey is now the "Snowdrop" centre of education and is not open to visitors.

Lorraine

Lorraine

Marville

The village of Marville is situated on a promontory in an attractive Country side and situated near to today's Belgium frontier. Marville today retains many important Historic links, situated 12 Kilometers east of Montmedy.

An Ancient site of Celtic worship where there during the Roman period stood a Roman villa and a Temple to Mars.

During the Merovingian period a Church was built on the site, Marville contains a Wealth of Ancient remains including Gothic and renaissance architecture. The Church of Saint Nicholas is a wonderful example of renaissance, architecture, carvings and statues.

For a century Marville was occupied by the Spanish from 1555, who built many beautiful renaissance buildings. In the vicinity of Marville there exists important sites of Merovingian archeology as of yet unexplored.

This modest village, built on the edge of the river Othain was once a flourishing town made wealthy by wool weaving and copper works. It became French with the Treaty of the Pyrenees . It's ramparts were razed and it was depopulated.

Some rich 16th and 17th Century houses in the Spanish style bear witness to its former glory: the houses of the weavers, the chevalier Michel, some cloth manufacturers, the Egremont Hotel.

The village is of Gallo-Roman origin. At the beginning of the 12th Century the land of Marville was given to the Abbey of Rebais by Audoenus the Frank, who established a Benidictine priory there. At the end of the 12th Century it belonged to the Count of Bar. It enjoyed the very rare privilege of being "common land" between the County of Bar and the Duchies of Lorraine and Luxembourg. This assured a long period of neutrality, from 1270 to 1659. At that date it became French territory by the Treaty of the Pyrenees.it was dismantled in 1677. Two Churches, a cemetery and twenty houses with sculpted facades are material evidence of its rich past.

The older of the two Churches, 500 metres away in the cemetery, is Saint Hilaire, which is a non vaulted 12th Century nave, although a parish existed there before 1227. The chapels, the ciborium above the side of the altar and its square choir, which is vaulted with pointed arches, are 14th Century. The nave is a veritable funeral museum made up of 16th-17th Century monuments raised from the cemetery. In the chapel of the Holy Sépulture there is a 14th Century Black marble altar and several tombstones under one of which lies the priest named; Hues, dated 1345.

The Church of Saint Nicolas, which unites both a 12th Century priory under the invocation of Saint Peter and a parish Church dating from 1227, which belongs to the Gothic period of the 14th Century. He blind nave of five spans flanked by aisles, of nds at anapse with five faces. Seven chapels open on the side aisles.

Lorraine

These are the confraternities and were erected between 1472 and 1536. The tower is above the first span. The organ loft includes a balcony in flamboyant style. The West door, which was remade in the 15th Century, is decorated on the inside with a Virgin and Child. In the side chapels, which are lit by a flamboyant network of windows, there are several remarkably 15th - 16th Century statues, altars with altarpieces and Gothic tabernacles and funeral monuments.

There was also a Capuchin Convent at Marville in 1618 and a Benedictine Monastery was established there in 1690 by the monks of Saint Nicolas.

The Church dates from the 13th and 14th Centuries. A statue of the Virgin greets you from above the great gateway. The nave is covered with a vault of pointed arches. Some chapels, constructed from the benevolence of wealthy patrons, open onto the aisles. A finely sculpted balustrade borders the loft. The Church is rich in statues, and two heavy cast iron stoops dating from the renaissance stand beside the entrance door.

Not far away, the cemetery of Saint Hilaire is hidden under gigantic fir trees. There huddled around the old Chapel are some tombs of the 15th, 16th, and 17th Centuries. The oldest part of the chapel dates back to the 11th Century and is rich in sculptures, tombstones and statues. At the bottom of the cemetery there is a strange ossuary decorated with small columns. The interior is deposited with 40.000 skulls, which are carefully arranged.

Lorraine

Lorraine

9

Saint Dagobert Fountain

At the heart of History, Legend and Nature…….

The Haut Charmois Estate goes back to at least Merovingian times, since the presence of a Gallo-Roman Villa, the remains of which are still to be discovered, is mentioned in ancient texts. By tradition, this was the first place that the body of Dagobert II was brought to.

King Dagobert II, thirteenth King of Austrasia, was threatened by Ebroin, who was the Mayor of the Palace to Thierry, King of Neustria. Ebroin administered Neustria unchecked and he wanted to seize Austrasia as well. Under the guidance of Wulfoad, his own Mayor of the Palace, Dagobert II has given his son Sigisbert a share of the throne.

But the King of Austrasia's sensible precautions were thwarted by Ebroin.

The year 679 was coming to its end and Dagobert was living in his Royal House, -SATHANACUM- known today as Stenay- where he was to spend the Christmas holiday. On December 23th, he went out hunting in the forest of "Wepria" (known today as Woevre) with a number of followers. Around the middle of the day, tired from the hunt, the King sat down near a fountain, which ran near a large oak, to take some rest. It is still called "ARPHIAS" and the section of the forest is known as "SCORTIA".

One of the servants among the conspirators struck the King while he was praying. Dagobert, the last King of a wide, powerful and peaceful realm, perished, dying while doing good.

Lorraine

The King's body was taken first to the site where now is the Château of Charmois, during the evening of December 23th, then to the Basilica of SATHANACUM, which at that time was dedicated to Saint Rémi. All the dignitaries of the realm came to mourn the death of the Sovereign.

A pilgrimage linked to the Holy King, assembling in as many as 36 parishes and passing through the forest to the Fountain of Saint Dagobert, was perpetrated without a break, from the 9th Century, until the revolution.

Today, the Saint Dagobert Pilgrimage includes a religious ceremony and a historical reminder, in the evening there are small festivities on the terrain of Château Charmois.

The pilgrimage takes place each year on the last Saturday of the month of August.

Lorraine

Brouennes

Brouennes is one of the most characteristic street-villages of the region, built alongside the Baalon stream. This small water-course has enabled ponds to be installed between the village and the Château of Bronelle to the west. In 1274 the village was gifted, under the Beaumont law, to Thibaut II, Count of Bar, some of its "furrows of land and a hovel" slipped from him and were given in perpetuity to Jehan de Chaufour, provost of Stenay.

Because of the many quarries in the area, many buildings, including some small chapels and the former Château of Givry, 1km to the North-East, are. Made of local stone, with its characteristic yellow color. This Château is privately owned and visits are not allowed. The families that owned the Château were the Ornés, the Aboncourt, the Lioncourt, the Strainchamps, then the Pouilly-Givry until 1817. Then the use of the Château became agricultural and all that remains now are the North-East tower of the chapel and several oval gunsights on a facade of the dependencies.

Lorraine

Quincy-Lands Ecourt

Archeological excavations have allowed Quincy's rich past to come to light. Numerous artifacts have been discovered and distributed around the museums in the region. At Quincy the oldest brewery of France can be found. The construction of the village goes back to 770 under Count Boson de Stenay. In 1287 four squires divided the village among themselves. They were Arnaud de Mont-Saint-Martin, his nephew Jean, Jeannot du Chauffour, and Clairambault de Flassigny. In 1415 the Château de Chaffour was dismantled, its ruins could still be seen up until the last century.

The village of Landzecourt was founded in 1109 by Gothelin de Lanza Court. It is situated on the right bank of the Loison, as Quincy is found on the left bank. The two villages were united in 1957.

Lorraine

Vigneault-Sous-Montmédy

In 1277 the village was gifted to Louis V, Count of Chiny and the Abbess of Juvigny. In 1657 during the siege of Montmedy, Louis XIV had set up his base in a field at Vigneault. Afterwards, this field was always known as the "King's Field". In fact, from this spot, the Citadel is actually visible. In the Church, it is worth looking at the stained glass windows of J. Henné, dating back from 1930, as well as those of Étienne and Mouilleron, made at Bar-le-Duc in 1901.

Lorraine

Charmois

This is an outpost of the Lorraine citadels of Stenay and Jametz, and opposite of Villefranche, à French citadel, opposite on the other side of the Meuse. Evidence of a Gallo-Roman presence was discovered under the courtyard of the higher Château (burned wooden structure, presence of tiles…).
In 1615, two brothers shared the estate, which explains the presence of two Châteaux so close together. Both buildings were originally surrounded by fortified farms. From the Middle Ages to the end of the 19th Century the Estate belonged to families of Charmoye and Herbemont.

In 1870, the old Château, or lower Château, was transformed into a troubadour style building. The village which surrounded it was razed.

The higher Château was turned into a farm. The building certainly dates back to before 1615, a date marked on the pediment of the entrance door. Built on a square plan, with four towers, there are two levels; on the courtyard side the first level is at two metres above ground level. For its defence it has numerous arrow slits on the towers, in the gatehouse to the right of the door, and to the inside.

After the French invasion in 1654, the frontier being now further away, windows were put in underneath the stone band. In 1870 the building was turned into a farm. The slope of the main roof was knocked down and the stone cornices on the main building removed to allow for hay windows to open. The gatehouse was also removed. The fireplace was taken down and the pieces of the fireplace were taken to the lower Château. In 1980, the Château was left virtually in ruins.

Since 1987 restoration works have been conducted by the new owners on the outbuildings, which were transformed into a gîte providing welcome to pilgrims who want to visit the Fountain of Dagobert in the forest.

Lorraine

Each year this Château hosts the feast of Saint Dagobert on the last Saturday of August, by organizing a medieval festival on their premises.

Lorraine

10
MEROVINGIAN FACTS

Merovingians got there name from there leader Merovee, they were first called the Franks after there King Frankus, and before that there name was; the Sicambrians after there Queen Cambra.

The origin of the Merovingian/Franks Royal House goes back to Troy/Greece.

After the fall of Troy they settled on the Black Sea around the Donau river.

They were eventually pushed westwards by the Goths and followed the Donau river into Pannonia, present day Hungary. There were several Frankish Kings/Dukes who have founded important European cities like Rotterdam, Frankfurt, Cologne, Brandenburg, Duisburg and Dresden, among others.

Frankus had assembled an army of 300.000 men to fight the Romans.

Merovingians had a mythical status in the ancient World.

Merovingian Kings were considered magicians, Priest/Kings.

When they traveled, they always used an oxcart.

One of the most important things for the Merovingian Kings was their hair, it was long and red and symbolisches their power and right to reign over their people.

They were married to multiple women at once and had many concubines to ensure offspring.

They had there own Royal Bodyguard, the Antrustions.

Lorraine

The language of there era was called Old Dutch.

Some of the more important figures in Frankish society also had high positions in the Roman Army and society and could speak the Latin language fluently.

They were fearsome fighters and had a special technique of throwing multiple axes at there enemy, the ax was called Franziska and weighed about 700 gram.

Whenever they went to war the treasure of the King was always carried with them, and so did the opponent.

Franks raided and fought in many countries as soldiers, as far as North Africa

They buried there Kings with Horses, Gold and Jewelry, the more powerful the King was the more Horses, Gold and Jewelry were buried with him, in the tomb of King Childeric in Tournai they found a total of 63 kilos of Gold and 15 Horses.

In the old days when a new King was crowned he was carried around on a shield as a celebration.

Anyone wishing to become a bodyguard (Antrustion) of a Merovingian King had to present himself fully armed to the King and with his hands in the King's hand had to swear an oath of allegiance to the King.

The "collapse" of the Rome Empire was a very gradual process where the Merovingian Kings already governed the lands in the name of Rome.

France was named after the Franks.

Lorraine

Paris is named after the forefather of the Merovingian Kings, "the famous Prince Paris, of Troy", Paris and Helena fame. That's why Paris is still called the city of love.

The people in this era of our European history were healthier then the people living before or after this period.

There were trade routes to many countries, England, Denmark, Norway and to the East as far as into India.

King Clovis married Clotilde, a Visigoth Princess; she was an Orthodox Christian, despite most of her own people, the Visigoth being Arian Christian.

Clovis converted to the Orthodox Christian faith after lengthy negotiations with the Bishop of Reims.

Clovis was crowned in Reims by the Bishop of Reims and was in fact the first Holy Roman Empire, his title was "the New Constantine", as head of the Church in his Kingdom.

The territories of the lands under control of the Merovingian Kings reached under Clovis as far as Hungaria, Frisia, Switzerland and Spain.

There were many marriages between Merovingian family members and Princes/Princesses from Thuringia, Burgundy and the Visigoth Kingdom.

The Roman Orthodox Church was struggling to survive in the early days.

King Clovis became the sword of the Roman Orthodox Christian Church.
There were two groups of Franks, the Salien Franks and the Ripurian Franks, they later merged into one group.

Merovingian craftsmanship was renowned in Europe.

Lorraine

They built many monasteries and Churches in there Kingdom.

Merovingian Kings appointed the Bischops of the Church.

They would rather be killed then to allow their hair to be cut.

Their administrative organisation was very decentralized.

Merovingian Kings didn't pay members of their staff, it was an honor to be working for the King.

Truth and Honor were great virtues in Merovingian times.

The sophistication of the Kingdom could rival that of Byzantium and other great civilizations.

The treasure of the King was considered the treasure of the people.

There is still a city in France that's called: Troy.

The Merovingian Kings Reigned, not Ruled over their people.

The Lords/Dukes of the Merovingian Kings were important men in the affairs of the Kingdom.

The Roman Catholic Church became more and more involved in politics in the Kingdom.

The Merovingian Kings had a warm relationship with the Eastern Orthodox Christian Church in Constantinople which was much more spiritual orientated.

The Majors of the Palace ruled the Kingdom in the name of the King. (Prime Minister).

Lorraine

The later Merovingian Kings managed a peaceful and prosperous Kingdom, they were later described as the do nothing Kings, but that was obviously politically motivated.

King Dagobert II's first wife was Mathilde from Thuringia, he was later married with Gisela of Razes (Rennes Le Château). Their son Sigisbert later became Count of Razes and was the ancestor of Godfried de Bouillon.

Most Royal Families in Europe can trace their lineage back to the Merovingians.

Lorraine

ABOUT THE AUTHORS

ORDER OF ANTRUSTIONS

The *Order of Antrustions* consist of a Select Group of individuals with a profound knowledge and sincere interest in the History of The Merovingian Bloodline,

The Ancient Heritage of this Sacred Bloodline, the origin of this Bloodline and its significance and relevance for Europe in our Modern Times.

The *Order of Antrustions* members all have Senior Positions in the Commercial and Financial sector, and have relevant Private Connections and Heritage regarding the Merovingian Bloodline.

The *Order of Antrustion*s will collect information regarding the Merovingian Bloodline from various sources, be it Public or Private, we have access to Private Records regarding the Merovingian Bloodline, there ancestors, offspring and their connections with the "Holy Family" and Ancient Egypt, and will publish this information on our Website for Members of the *Order of Antrustions*.

www.antrustions.com

Lorraine

Afterword

The Order of Antrustions collects information from various sources regarding the Merovingian Bloodline. This Bloodline is still present in our modern day society and in our opinion is still very relevant today.

If you are anxious to learn more about the Order of Antrustions visit our website and become a member, you will have access to all our publications and (depending on your membership level) are invited to participate in lectures and field trips we organize to places of interest connected to the Sacred Merovingians.

In the following pages you will find an introduction to our other publications. These Books can be ordered on the Order of Antrustions Amazon page. You can find the link on our website or visit us directly on www.amazon.com.

www.antrustions.com

Lorraine

Knights Templars, the Merovingian Connection

One of the most remembered and famous first Crusaders was certainly Godfried de Bouillon, he and his brother Baldwin of Bourges, with other family members, who were of Merovingian descent. Baldwin would become the first King of Jerusalem, which was his rightful title.

The Merovingian bloodline of Dagobert II, through his son Sigisbert IV, came to Godfroi de Bouillon, who captured Jerusalem in 1099. His niece, Melusine, of Godfroi (1061-1100) married Foulques V, count of Anjou whose son, Geffrey Plante Genest, fathered the Plantagenet Kings of England.

The Kingdom of Jerusalem had its origins in the First Crusade, when proposals to govern the city as an ecclesiastical state were rejected.

Lorraine

Abbey of Jouarre

The history of the abbey reaches as far back into the Seventh Century. There then lived at Ussy-sur-Marne, a well-known family whose members had important posts in the service of the Merovingian Kings of that time. Because of their position they probably received land and properties, amounting to quite a fortune.

Three brothers of this family, sons of Autharius, known as Adon, Radon and Dadon. The children were all born at Sancy near Soissons in the first years of the Seventh Century, somewhere around 603-606.

They were all being blessed by St. Columbanus around 610-611, and were still very young when they entered the service of King Clotaire II to be trained to enter into high functions at the palace of the King.

Order of Antrustions

Lorraine

Pharamund
Chlodion
Mérovée
Childeric
Clovis

From Francs to Merovingians

Early Germanic society, which was patriarchal in character, was based on clan groupings, emphasizing warrior values and was socially divided into different levels: nobles, free warriors, and slaves. War Kingship and war bands were a dynamic force at the time when the Franci and other confederations (Alemani) appeared in Germany.

The pre-Migration Germanic tribes consisted of people whose sense of unity came from legends of common ancestry and the value of pure blood. The leader, a man of noble lineage linked to divine ancestors, was a Long Haired King (Reges Criniti) and he was the guarantor of law, social order, fertility, and peace. In Germanic society, religion dominated every aspect of life, including power.

Their long hair was the essential and venerated symbol of legitimacy, sacral powers and divine right to reign. The King was therefore recognized by his people as a descendant of the Gods, and was the mediator between the realm of men and the Gods, as a Priest King.

A tribal chief was chosen to lead his tribe into war and was chief of eager young warriors (a comitatus). This now had become by the third century the template of a new kind of Kingship and in doing so also provided for a new kind of cultural identity.

The complicated events of the fifth century, which eventually led to the breakup of the Roman Empire in the west, served to enhance this new sense of Frankish identity. Other then barbarian peoples such as the Huns, originating from the Asian steppes, or for instance the Visigoths, fighting and plundering for over forty years, the Franks had no vast migration to make.

Already well established in their German homeland, straddling the Lower Rhine and divided into many different competing groups, their war leaders expanded their power as circumstances permitted them to do so.

A small garrison occupying the fort of Vieux-Moulin, overlooking the Meuse, between 370 AD and 450 AD was a symbol of this relative stability in a fastly changing world.

Lorraine

Antrustions
Bodyguards of Merovingian Kings

The Kings Leudes "Antrustions" were framed from the start as a particular class, contributed with broad lawful benefits, their points of interest were, the odds of fortune and influence. This turns out to be a consistently expanding pre-prominence and a pre-distinction, having a tendency to get innate. It is in this manner, that the class of Antrustions, without considering the starting point or any lawful condition, brought forth present day honorability.

As the King was acquainted with the customs of the Romans, from the Antrustions there were many offices. The highest rank was Major Domus who was next to the King and appointed by the King, but in 641 the nobles had acquired the right to appoint him, "which led to the rise of Charles Martel and the Carolingians".

Order of Antrustions

Lorraine

Sigisbert III

Son of Dagobert I, father of Dagobert II

He was the son of Ragnetrude (or Raintrude) and Dagobert I. Baptized by Saint Armand about a month after his birth, he would have, according to legend himself, answered aloud "Amen" to the blessing.

Proclaimed King of Austrasia at the age of 9, after the death of his father in 649, Sigisbert III governed his Kingdom with the help of several advisers: Pepin de Landen, former Mayor of the Palace of Dagobert I, Saint Cunibert of Cologne and Grimoald, son by Pepin the Elder.

Very pious, he favored the progression of Christianity by sending missionaries to areas of his Kingdom that remained pagan. According to tradition King Sigisbert is at the origin of 12 to 20 monasteries. We know for sure that he founded in the Ardennes those of Cugnon, Malmedy and Stavelot.

He married Princess Mathilde who in 651 gave him a son, Dagobert II after a reign of 23 years, Sigisbert III died on February 1, 656, from a short illness. According to his will, his body was placed in the crypt of the Church of the Abbey of Saint-Martin-Devant-Metz.

Order of Antrustions

Lorraine

A Sacred Bloodline

To understand the complete History of the Sacred Merovingian Bloodline we have to trace the origins of this Bloodline back to the very beginning. This origin starts in Arcadia (Greece). The next stage in their History is the legendary city of Troy. After the destruction of Troy the surviving inhabitants went to find other places to settle, as the area of the western coast of the Black Sea, Butrint, Rome etc.

They ruled over the Scithians, but were eventually pushed west by the Huns. Following the Donau river they eventually ended up by following the Rhine river into the Low Countries, (first Germany and later the Netherlands) where they founded the first settlements, among others a settlement called Rotta (Rotterdam). After being pushed out of this region by the Romans they were allowed to settle in Tournai, Belgium where they served as local chiefs (Dukes) under the Romans.

When the influence of Rome in the North of Francia gradually diminished, the Merovingian Kings (especially Clovis) were able to fully control and expand their Empire to the whole of Francia, (present day France) and large parts of Germany, Belgium, Switzerland and the Netherland, with Paris as there Capital, (named in honor of there ancestor the Trojan Prince, Paris).

The Merovingians ruled much of present-day France and Germany between the fifth and seventh centuries. The beginning of this time coincides with not only the Grail stories, but with the era of King Arthur, who was so central to many of these tales.

There was never any question that the Merovingians were the rightful rulers of the Franks. They were not "created" as kings. The sons who were entitled became Kings automatically on their twelfth birthdays.

Their role was not to govern - that was left to the "Mayors of the Palace."

Lorraine

Order of Antrustions

Lorraine

Merovingian Kings

Numerous small Frankish Kingdoms existed during the 5th century around Cologne, Tournai, Le Mans, Cambrai, and elsewhere. Dispargum castrum (near Duisburg, Germany) served as the base camp for conquests by the Frankish warriors.

The battle-proven Chlodio (son of Pharamond) felt strong enough after about two years of preparation to cross the Rhine and move further west (today's Belgium). For a long time, the Franconia Alliance was one of the most reliable allies in Rome, before the Franks subjugated almost all of Gaul in the west and the Alemanni, Thuringia, Burgundy and Bavaria in the east. Other tribal areas and especially Roman cities were there for looting and pillaging.

Tournai had been a Roman garrison-town of some importance, and its trade and industry had helped to supply the needs of the legions stationed on the Lower Rhine. It had suffered under the Vandals in 407.

The Salien francs were defeated near Arras by Aetius and Majorien (Roman emperor from 457 to 461). Although defeated and submissive, Clodion was entrusted by Rome with the command of the Roman-Frankish troops in Belgium.

The Kingdom of Chlodio in Tournai eventually came to dominate its neighbours, most likely because of its association with Aegidius, the magister militum of Northern Gaul. A Frankish King, Childeric I, fought with Aegidius in 463. Childeric I and his son Clovis I were both commanders of the Roman military in the Province of Belgica Secunda and were subordinate to the magister militum.

Lorraine

Order of Antrustions

Lorraine

Antrustions Notebook

The Order of Antrustions has created a Merovingian Notebook which can be used for different purposes, like notes on ideas, appointments and other information you feel necessary to write down. Every page has an inspirational quote or a fact connected to Merovingian History and or Wisdom.

Order of Antrustions

Lorraine

History of Dagobert II

Son of the Merovingian King Sigisbert III, grandson of King Dagobert I, he was born around 652 AD. When his father died in 663, he was exiled by Grimoald, the Mayor of the palace, and was educated in a monastery in Ireland.

However, Grimoald's treacherous ruse was to no avail. When Wilfred, Bishop of York, told the lords of Austrasia of the existence of their King, they called him back to the throne in 675. After he had taken his country Austrasie back, Dagobert II brought peace and stability, and founded numerous churches and abbeys.

Saint Dagobert II
Merovingian King

In 679, a conflict broke out with Neustria. Thierry was their King and his Mayor of the Palace, Ebroin, conceived a plot against Dagobert, who was then assassinated on 23rd December 679, in the forest of' Woëvre, some distance from his royal summer palace in Stenay.

After the death of Dagobert II, the Merovingian bloodline continued in the personage of the son of Dagobert II, SigisbertIV, who, together with his mother Gisèle of Razes fled to the South of France, to the village of Rennes le Chateau in Razes where his grandfather Béra II the Count of Razès lived.

Order of Antrustions

Lorraine

Lorraine

Order of Antrustions
The Netherlands
2020

Lorraine

Closing Argument

We feel that writing books about the Merovingians and there present day family connections is needed.

Surely there are already enough publications about the subject of the Merovingians, and although this is true, never has the whole story about the Merovingian correctly been told, much of the publications upon till now are either fragmented or incorrect.

Our aim is to provide historically correct documents with in-depth knowledge of the facts, to give our readers a greater understanding of the structure, motives and struggles of the different parties involved and how this period in our history has shaped our present society.

Merovingian Kings were spiritual guides for their people, whoever had a problem, of whatever nature, could ask for an audience with the King and discuss the issue, and he would be given advice, guidance and if needed, healing. They were truly Priest/Kings as signified by there long hair, which is a very ancient custom, going back thousands of years.

Beware!

Once you're entering through this history door you will find that this knowledge will capture your full- time attention or none at all. If you become a seeker of truth, your friends might see you as becoming a little strange. Indeed, what would they think of you? Strange behavior, muttering about Ancient History, the Good and the Righteous, and Chemistry.

Things most people simply don't think about.

Lorraine

The Merovingians are an interesting story unto themselves, having been really the first rulers of what we now identify as France. They established a cultural identity that lives to this day and remnants of their influence can still be seen in the laws, mores, architecture, and language. The rule that was established by them was the precursor to feudalism, they were supporting the early Catholic Church. Many Merovingians became prominent church leaders and/saints.

This was the seed of a long and deep nationalism that affects the world upon today.

"We have to understand why there has been, until now, not much information available for the general public regarding this important period in our Western European History."

This time in our European History was the decisive period in the establishment of the Holy Roman Catholic Church as the dominant Power in Europe for the next 1000 year.

We sincerely hope you will enjoy and learn from our publications!

With the highest respect:

Order of Antrustions

Printed in Great Britain
by Amazon